BERWICK

A Short History and Guide

by

FRANK GRAHAM

First published by Frank Graham
Published by Butler Publishing in 1987
Reprinted
© 1987   ISBN 0946928 16 9

BUTLER PUBLISHING
Thropton, Morpeth, Northumberland NE65 7LP

Printed by Crescent Printing Company
195 Alexandra Road, Ashington, Northumberland NE63 9LA

W. Armstrong's Map
1769

From Edinburgh

From Eyemouth

From Dunse

Lammermoor Hills

Lamerton

Sweetmilk Hall 3

Marshall Medon (Balderw

Nunlees

Hay Esq'. Mordington

New Farm

Sedgeburn

Steps o

Edrington glafsCha'

Boundary Ho:

Bower

West Edge

Gairfield 2

Hows Hall

BERWICK

ruins

BatesCrofs Cocklan

Farm

Hallydown Hill

Battle 1333

Brow

Conundrum

Sons and Seal

Barnet Esq'

Mount Pleasant

Num'. One

Greves stead

Mount

BOUNDS

Latham

1

River

From Kyloe

Mills Hill

Faimy Flatts

New Water

W Mill

ruins

Fort

B

Paxton n Esq'

Gaens law

Compton Esq'

Twee

edmouth

Fish Houses

Jn W' Blackett B'

West Ord

Kettleby

Ed. mouth

Spittle

Bank House

New Water House

Loan Head

East Ord

Common

Horn Cliff Alder Esq'

Longridge

Mid. Ord

Herds House

Ord Moor

Priors

Mains

Velvett Hall

Billy law

Ord Moor

Pitt House

2

Coal

O

U

N

Morton

Cuckholds Square

West Hill

Hill

East Field

Thornton

Engine

Jn W' Blackett Bar'

Unthank

3

West Field

Carmel Esq'

Coal House

Stone House

Hill

4

Shorswood

Allerdean

Folly

O

F

Moor

BERWICK

Berwick is one of Britain's most historic towns, picturesquely situated at the northern apex of Northumberland. Approached from the south it presents a striking appearance on the north bank of the Tweed. Within the narrow confines of the town are more buildings of historic and artistic interest than can be found elsewhere in the British Isles. As yet the town has escaped the era of concrete and plastic and has not yet been sacrificed to the motor car. There are good signs that this will continue since the town has a strong civic pride and the London developers do not yet see it as a place to ravage and exploit.

The town was most probably founded by the Saxons but in those days would be of little importance as compared with Bamburgh which was a royal city. The name, which literally means "corn farm", suggests a small agricultural settlement.

The first authentic notice of Berwick is a charter of Edgar, King of Scotland, conferring the village in 1097 on the Bishop of Durham. During the reign of King David of Scotland (1124-1153) it became a Scottish royal burgh. During the years that were to follow Berwick changed hands between England and Scotland thirteen times. In 1214 it was laid waste by King John but quickly recovered. In the reign of Alexander III (1247-1286) it reached the height of its prosperity, the Lanercost Chronicle describing it as a city so populous and of such commercial importance that it might justly be called another Alexandria, whose riches were the sea and the water was its walls. In 1286 the customs of Berwick amounted to £2,190 annually paid into the Scottish Exchequer. The customs of the whole of England were only four times as large.

When in 1292 Edward I gave Scotland to Baliol in the great hall of Berwick Castle eighty substantial burghers of Berwick took the oath of allegiance to Edward. But in 1296 war broke out between the two kingdoms and Berwick was the first to suffer. About 7,000 of the inhabitants were massacred. The last to hold out were a body of Flemings, who had done much to develop the trade of the town. They held out in the "Red Hall of Commerce" until it was destroyed by fire. The town was ruined and the greatest merchant-city of Northern Britain sank from that time into a petty seaport. It was re-peopled with English traders and the remnants of the Scots who swore allegiance to the King. The Countess of Buchan who had crowned Bruce at Scone was kept in a cage in Berwick Castle where for four years she was exposed to public view.

We need not describe in detail the battles that were fought over Berwick for the following decades. Early in the fourteenth century the town walls were built and English merchants encouraged to settle. During the Wars of the Roses Berwick was given to Scotland in return for help against the Yorkists. For twenty-one years it remained in their hands, but in 1482 an English army took the town without any resistance being offered and thereafter it remained in English hands.

The town was a county in itself and not part of Northumberland. The "bounds" include an area of eight square miles. At the north end is Lamberton Toll where for many years, as at Gretna, runaway couples were married. The peculiarly independent position of Berwick is explained by the following humorous legend:

"During the temptation while the Evil One was showing to the Holy One all the kingdoms of the earth, he kept Berwick hidden beneath his thumb, wishing to reserve it as his own little nook".

The Old Bridge

The lovely old bridge with its red sandstone weathered for more than 300 years is one of the sights of Berwick. The first bridge was a hundred yards higher up the river and was built of wood. In the reign of King John, we read, "the bridge at Berwick broke with great force of water, because the arches of it were low". It was restored by William, King of Scotland. We are told that James VI of Scotland was worried about crossing this wooden structure on his journey south to be crowned James I of Great Britain. "Is there ne'er a man in Berwick", he is alleged to have said, "whae can boo (work) stanes to mak' a brig ower the Tweed?" Whether the story is true or not, work on a new bridge was started in 1610. Progress was very slow and it wasn't until 1624 that the bridge was completed at a cost of £15,000. John Fuller's description in 1799 still applies today. "It is built", he writes, "of fine hewn stone, and has fifteen spacious and elegant arches. It measures 1,164 feet in length, including the land stalls. Its width is seventeen feet. At each of the pillars, which are fourteen in number, there is an outlet to both sides; without these there would be much greater danger either in walking or riding along the bridge than there is at present. The sixth pillar separates Berwick from the county Palatine of Durham. The battlements at the outlets at this pillar are always covered with sods as a guide to constables and others in the execution of warrants for the apprehension of delinquents (the pillar is still distinguished by having battlements higher than the others). The fourth gate of the town, together with the adjoining guard-house, shut up the bridge at its northern extremity. Towards the middle of it there are two strong wooden barriers 148 feet distant from each other. In order to give additional security to this mode of defence, they are made to project considerably beyond the battlements".

The quality of the workmanship in building the bridge is shown in the fact that after three hundred and fifty years it still stands as strong as ever.

Royal Border Bridge

The Royal Border Bridge, one of the finest railway viaducts in the world, was built in three years between 1847 and 1850. It was designed by Robert Stephenson. Two thousand workmen were employed and the total cost was £253,000. It is an imposing structure of twenty-eight arches, stands 126 feet above water level and is 720 yards long. The arches contain 1,710,000 bricks.

BIRDS EYE VIEW OF BERWICK FROM THE SOUTH

Royal Tweed Bridge

This modern bridge which now carries the main road north spans the river with four big arches. The northern span is 361 feet making it the longest concrete span in the country. When it was being built a bed of peat was discovered at the foundations of one of the piers. One hundred and eighty-six concrete piles, each thirty-six feet long and weighing two tons, were used to provide a solid bed. The bridge is a very heavy structure lacking in elegance, a fact which is conspicuous because it stands beside two magnificent earlier structures.

Union Chain Bridge

Four miles up the Tweed from Berwick is the Union Chain Bridge. When describing the three Berwick bridges we feel it appropriate to mention this famous structure. It was erected by Captain S. Brown, R.N. in 1820. Its total length between the points of suspension is 432 feet, its width eighteen feet, and its height above low water sixty-nine feet. It is built of malleable iron of a total weight of only 100 tons. A contemporary thus describes it:-

"The new iron suspension-bridge over the Tweed at this point, is one of the greatest acquisitions the country possesses, and at the same time one of the finest specimens in existence of modern invention employed as a medium of social and commercial intercourse. The daily inconvenience—besides serious accidents and loss of life—to which the inhabitants were so long subjected, has thus been completely remedied; it admits two carriages abreast, affords the usual accommodation for foot passengers, and has proved of incalculable benefit to the public".

THE OLD BRIDGE   *Photograph courtesy of Berwick-upon-Tweed Borough Council*

Berwick Castle

Little is left of what was once one of the most important of the Border castles. Almost all that was standing of the fortress was destroyed over a century ago to make way for the Railway Station. The Great Hall of the Castle in which Edward I in 1292 declared in favour of Baliol as king of Scotland corresponds with the present station platform.

The castle has witnessed many stirring events in Border history, changing hands on more than one occasion, its history being closely linked with the fortified town of Berwick. In 1377 it was seized by seven intrepid Borderers who slew the governor, Sir Robert Boynton. They were joined by forty-one more confederates and held out for eight days against 10,000 English soldiers. Their heroism was not respected by their enemies since on surrendering the castle they were all put to the sword.

After the Union of the two kingdoms the castle decayed. In 1762 it is described as follows: "It is environed on one side by the ditch of the town; on the other by one of the same breadth, flanked by many round towers and thick walls, which enclose a large palace, in the middle of which rises a lofty keep or donjon, capable of a long resistance, and commanding all the environs of the town".

The remains of the castle which survive are the White Wall and a flight of steps nearby which lead down to the Water Tower.

Berwick Town Walls

Berwick is famous for its two sets of town walls. The first, of which only fragments remain, was built by Edward II, and was two and a half miles long; the second, which is the glory of Berwick, dates from the early years of Elizabeth, and is a mile and three-quarters in length.

The medieval walls were begun by Edward I; at least the ditch outside was dug by him; the wall was built by Edward II, and strengthened by Bruce about 1320. It had nineteen towers and five gates and in Henry VIII's time was twenty-two feet high. The wall had an earthen embankment behind which was a retaining wall, forming the "Countermore". Entrance to the towers was through the Countermore by a narrow passage supported by timber.

The old wall began at the Mary Gate where a short road led to the castle. It went to the Bell Tower and along the line of the wall that is still visible to the Brass Mount. The Bell Tower is not the original but an Elizabethan replacement. Its rounded base is medieval. A stone's throw away can be seen Lord Soulis Tower (also called Lord's Mount) which was begun in Edward's reign and finished in that of Mary, 1555. This is the northeast angle of the Edwardian walls. Lord Soulis was a supporter of Bruce, and was appointed Governor of Berwick. He rebelled against the king, was captured and imprisoned. This was the time when Berwick was controlled by Scotland. From the Brass Mount the medieval wall followed close to the line of the Elizabethan Wall except that the Elizabethan Wall did not take in the area of the Ness. After Meg's Mount the Edwardian wall continued to the castle. There was a gap between the Percy Tower and the Mary Gate which was covered by the castle.

When the Elizabethan walls were built guns, not arrows, dominated warfare. They were built on a new Italian system of bastions which had not been tried out in the north. The Berwick bastions were designed by an engineer, Portinari, and probably by Jacopo a Contio, who was certainly consulted. The diagram explains how the bastions work. They are designed to give fire cover for every part of the wall. They consist of a platform facing the attacker with an obtuse angle connected to the curtain wall by a narrow collar. The recesses between the platform, collar and wall are called flankers. They contained guns which fired through embrasures. The flankers were accessible by means of tunnels. The wall was ten to twelve feet thick backed by a mound of earth thirty feet thick. Soon after the wall was built the bastions were filled with mounds of earth above the level of the stonework and called "cavaliers". Because of this the bastions were often called "Mounts".

Outside the curtain wall, as well as round the bastions, there was a ditch 200 feet in width, and in the midst of this another ditch twelve feet broad and eight feet deep, kept always full of water. Originally a sentry walk ran right round the wall but this was later covered to form the present rampart. Guns could be mounted on the slope behind.

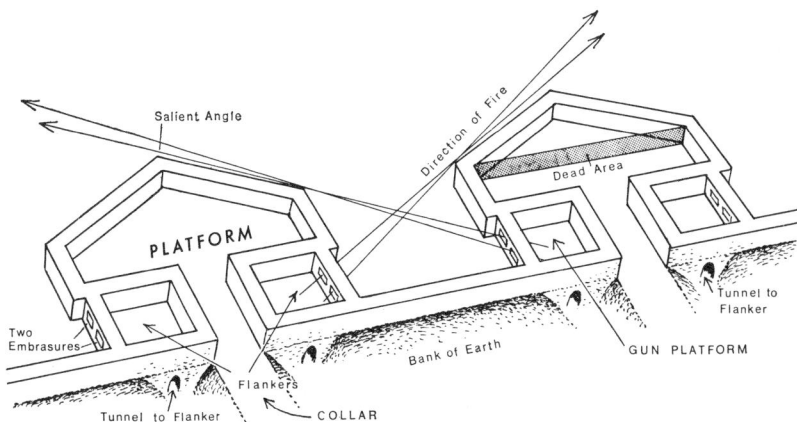

Salient Angle

Direction of Fire

Dead Area

PLATFORM

Two Embrasures

Tunnel to Flanker

Flankers

Bank of Earth

Tunnel to Flanker

GUN PLATFORM

COLLAR

The Gates

There are four gates. The most conspicuous is *Scotsgate*. The original gate was smaller and single arched. The present structure replaced it in the early nineteenth century. Until the battle of Waterloo this gate was locked at 10 p.m. each night. The only original gate remaining is the *Cowport* which has portcullis grooves and a massive wooden door. As its name implies this gate was used by the citizens to lead their cattle out to pasture. Opposite is a redoubt called the *Great Bulwark in the Snook*, which is surrounded by a deep ditch. The *Ness Gate* was built in 1816, to give access to the new pier. The *Shore Gate*, with its huge wooden doors, dates from the seventeenth century. In front of the Brass Bastion can be seen the Batardean, a low wall controlling the water in the moat. From the King's Mount the Catwell Wall ran across to Bridge Street (the Edwardian Wall followed the waterside right round). A section of it can be seen behind a baker's shop. From the King's Mount a round projection shows where the Edwardian Black Watch Tower used to stand.

In the eighteenth century the Catwell Wall was abandoned and fortifications were built along the riverside as far as the old bridge. Fisher's Fort contains a gun captured at Sebastopol. Next comes Four Gun Battery (also called Bramham's Battery) which as its name implies has four stone platforms and embrasures. Coxon's Tower probably incorporates the Edwardian "New Tower".

The fortifications of Berwick were dismantled in 1819.

Town Gate ~Berwick.

The Cowgate (about 1920)

Drawn by A Clarke ;   *Engraved by R Scott*

Berwick Church. 1799

Drawn by A. Carse.   *Engraved by R. Scott.*

High Street and Town Hall from Main Guard.   1799

Main Guard

This building, now on the Palace Green, used to stand in Marygate, near the *Advertiser* office. In 1799 it is described as follows:- "It is most incommodiously placed in the High Street, 100 yards distant from the Scotch Gate, the spot where it should have stood. It consists of a room for the officer of the guard, a large apartment in the middle of the house for the soldiers, with benches for them to lye upon. There is likewise a large fire place in it. Besides it has an apartment called the black-hole". In 1816 it was removed to the Palace Green.

The Parish Church

The parish church dedicated to the Holy Trinity, and built by John Young of London, is one of the only two churches dating from Commonwealth times (the other being Staunton Harold in Lincolnshire). The materials of which it is constructed, like the Barracks and Border Bridge, were obtained from the old castle. It is quadrangular in shape and built in a simple, almost plain, style. It is a building of great architectural interest. The west doorway is flanked by two big buttresses and two turrets (dating from the nineteenth century). There are two fine arcades of semi-circular arches, resting on slender round pillars. The panelled oak pulpit is Elizabethan and belonged originally to the old parish church at St. Mary's Gate. John Knox is said, by tradition, to have preached from it when in Berwick in 1548. The most valuable glass in the church is in the west window.

It has twenty-five medallions of seventeenth century Flemish workmanship. This stained glass was brought from the chapel of the Duke of Buckingham at Canons Park, London.

BERWICK CHURCH.
North
Published 1 June 1824 by W. Davison, Alnwick

13

Town Hall

The Town Hall stands on the site of two previous tolbooths. The architects were Samuel and John Worrall, the contractors Pattison and Dods, the last of whom has his name above the door – "J. Dods, Architect". It is a fine example of Georgian architecture. The principal features are the portico and steeple. The former consists of four Tuscan columns supporting a handsome pediment, on which are engraved the arms of the town. The ground floor is enriched with an arcade. The steeple rises to a height of 150 feet and contains eight bells, one of which is rung as a curfew every night, except Sunday, at eight o'clock. A century ago not only did the Council meet here but the courts, police station and gaol were all in the same building. The gaol was described in the eighteenth century as "perhaps the most healthy and pleasant one in the kingdom, with excellent views of the town, the German Ocean, Bambro' Castle and Holy Island". The well preserved cells can still be seen. The chamber where the Quarter Sessions were held has been turned into fine public assembly rooms.

The Town Hall is so much more ecclesiastical in appearance than the parish church that it has often been mistaken for it. "The parish church", one writer remarks, "is a mean structure in Cromwell's time, and is without either tower or bell; and the people are summoned to divine service from the belfry of the Town Hall, which has a very respectable steeple. Indeed, so much more ecclesiastical in appearance is the Town Hall than the church, that a regiment of soldiers, on the first Sunday after their arrival at Berwick, marched to the former building for divine service although the church stood opposite the barrack-gate. A strange clergyman one Sunday morning was seen trying the Hall door and rating the absent sexton. He had become involved in the same mistake as the soldiers".

The Barracks

The imposing barracks were probably designed by Vanbrugh and the work carried out by A. Jelf. They were the first barracks built in Britain and were erected as a result of protests by the townspeople who had the burdensome task of billeting the soldiers. We are told that when the building was completed the Board of Ordnance had no money left for utensils and furniture. The keepers of the alehouses raised sufficient money to save having the soldiers quartered on them. It is a striking building. The massive gate-house is capped by a coat of arms and has fine ornamental iron gates. Across the courtyard is the main building, crow-gabled, with a recessed arch above the clock. Inside is a Regimental Museum. Until recently the Barracks were the joint depot of the Royal Scots and King's Own Scottish Borderers making them the oldest occupied barracks in the country.

Drawn by J. Cleve.   Engraved by R. Love.

The Barracks.   1799

The Pier

In the sixteenth century with the increased trade of the town the harbour mouth, always difficult to enter, was causing considerable trouble. To improve the entrance a pier was erected in 1577 at a cost of £700. By 1810 it was in a ruinous condition and it was decided to replace it. The work took eleven years and cost £60,000. The total length is 960 yards. A few years later, in 1826, a lighthouse was erected at the end. The lighthouse now shows a white light flashing every five seconds and is visible for twelve miles. The pier is a popular promenade and a place for watching the salmon fishing.

The King's Arms Hotel - Berwick

Inns

In 1799 we are told there were fifty-nine public houses and three coaching inns in Berwick, namely the Red Lion in the High Street, the King's Arms in Hide Hill, and the Hen and Chicken in Sandgate. The Red Lion which appears to have been the most important has now disappeared. It was at the King's Arms that Dickens stayed in 1861 when he gave a reading in the Assembly Rooms attached to the hotel. Looking up Hide Hill the King's Arms Hotel "makes a fine picture. It is designed just like a typical Georgian country house". The Hen and Chicken is a substantial stone building of three storeys.

Grammar School

The former Grammar School stands in Palace Street East. It is three storeys high of six bays. Built in 1754, "in the cheapest and best manner possible", it was in use as a school until 1820 when a new building was erected.

Governor's House

The Governor of Berwick was in charge of the garrison of the town. He resided on the Palace Green. The fine eighteenth century building is now partly used by the Ministry of Pensions. It is three storeys high with five bays and two-storey wings. The angle bays in front are flanked by tall pilasters.

The Avenue

Drawn by Joseph Lycett, Berwick.

Engraved by R. Scott.

East View of the Governor's House. 1799

PLAN of BERWICK
-1745-

Shewing line of Old Fortifications
erected ·1310 — 1320
also present walls
built about 1560.

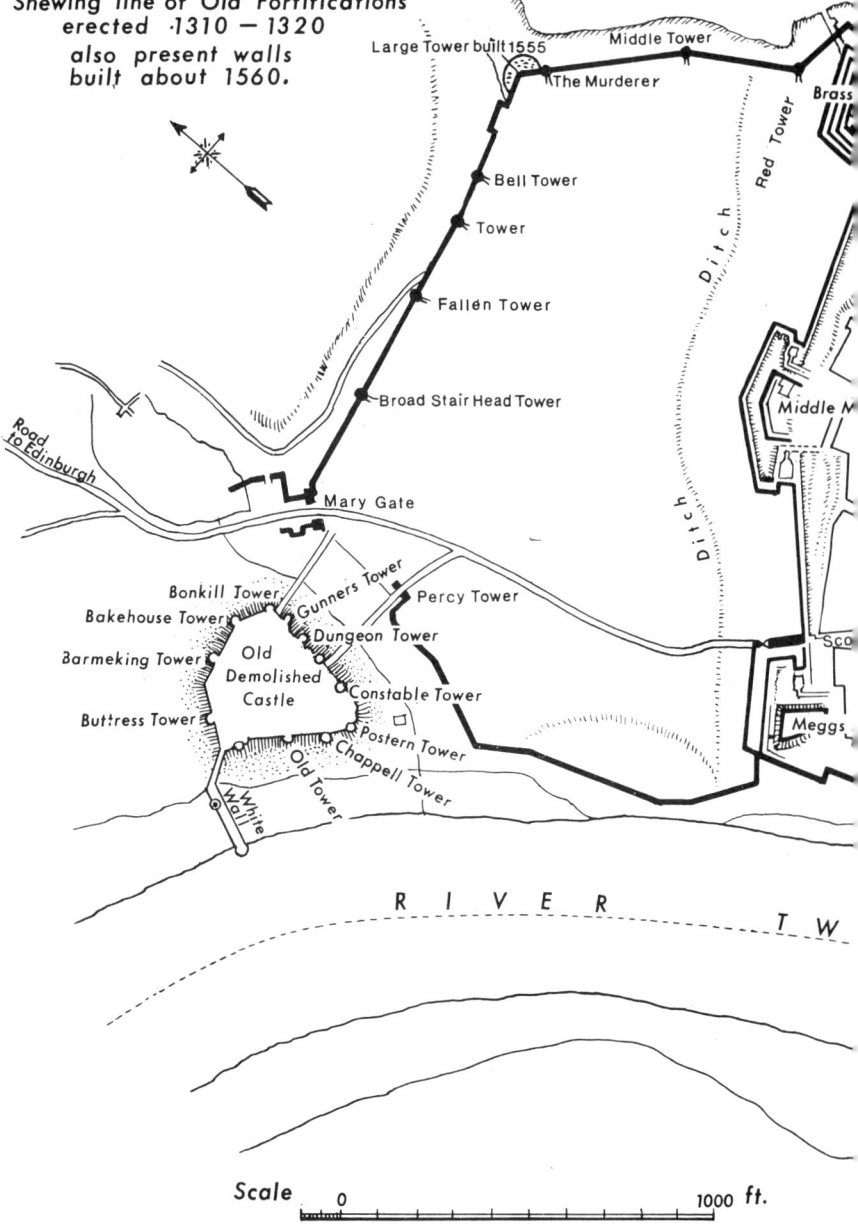

Large Tower built 1555

Middle Tower

The Murderer

Brass

Bell Tower

Tower

Red Tower

Ditch

Fallen Tower

Broad Stair Head Tower

Middle M

Road to Edinburgh

Ditch

Mary Gate

Gunners Tower

Percy Tower

Bonkill Tower

Bakehouse Tower

Dungeon Tower

Sco

Barmeking Tower

Old Demolished Castle

Constable Tower

Buttress Tower

Postern Tower

Meggs

White Wall

Old Tower

Chappell Tower

R I V E R   T W

Scale   0   1000 ft.

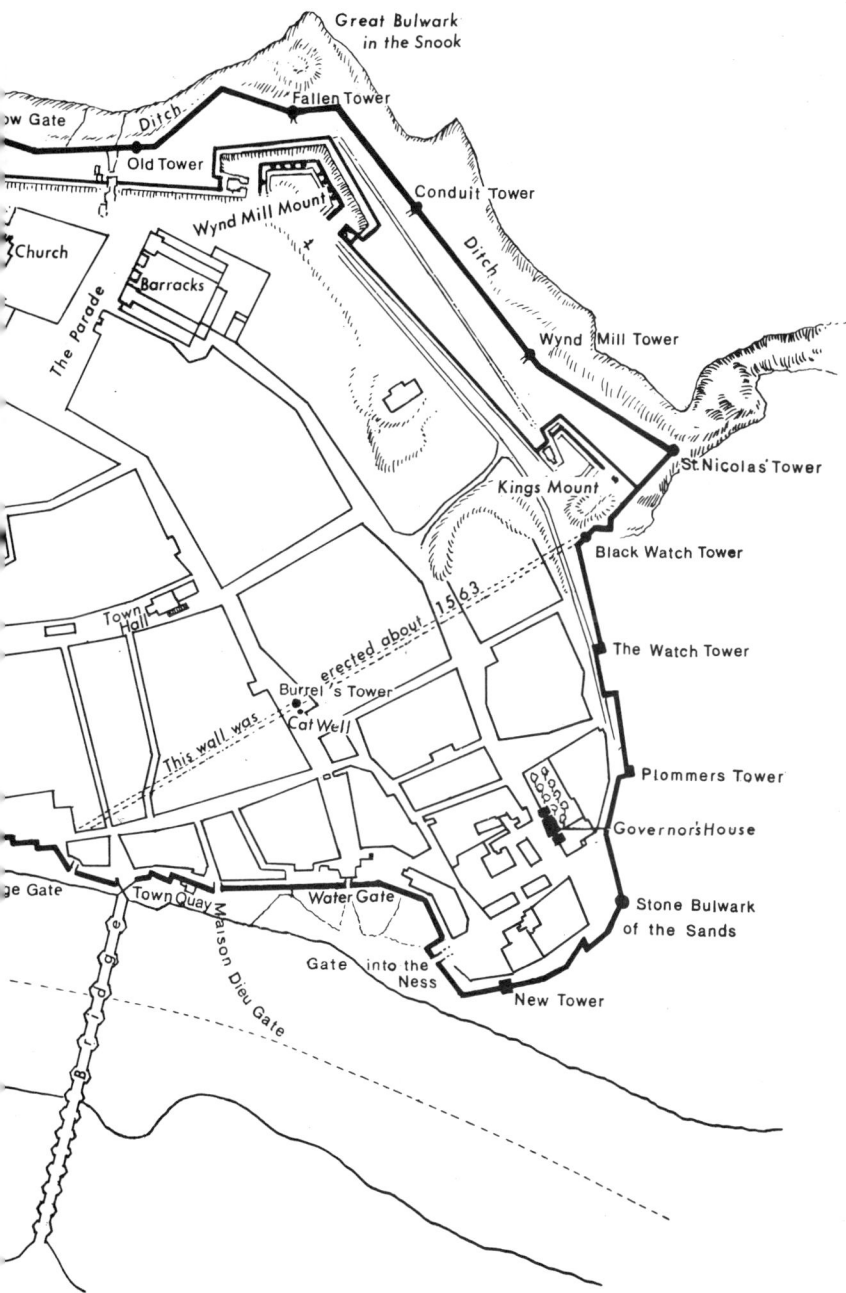

Great Bulwark
in the Snook

ow Gate | Ditch | Fallen Tower

Old Tower

Conduit Tower

Church

Wynd Mill Mount

The Parade

Barracks

Ditch

Wynd Mill Tower

Kings Mount

St Nicolas' Tower

Black Watch Tower

erected about 1563

The Watch Tower

Town Hall

This wall was

Burrel's Tower

Cat Well

Plommers Tower

Governor's House

ge Gate | Town Quay

Water Gate

Maison Dieu Gate

Stone Bulwark
of the Sands

Gate into the Ness

New Tower

Vicarage

This stately old house stands in Church Street. Built in 1749 it is a five-bay brick house with segment-headed windows.

Golden Square

Part of the street which leads from the Royal Tweed Bridge into Marygate is old. At the north-west end is the former Corporation Academy built in 1800. It is a simple four-bay building. It was built by the Town Guild because the Grammar School was failing to meet the educational needs of the town.

Custom House

The Quay Walls is one of the finest streets in Berwick. Among its interesting buildings is the Custom House built late in the eighteenth century, an outstanding example of Georgian architecture. It is two storeys high with five bays, with arched windows on the first floor and a Venetian doorway with foliated pilasters.

It was once the Dispensary, the first health institution in Berwick.

Custom House, Berwick · 18th Cent.

THE OLD JAIL

Photograph courtesy of Berwick-upon-Tweed Borough Council

Palace Street

Wellington Terrace, Berwick.

One of the fine houses still remaining in Berwick, No. 1 Wellington Terrace, has harpoon heads carved on the front door showing it was originally built for someone connected with the whaling trade.

Hide Hill. 1799

THE OLD STOCKS — last used 1857

Photograph courtesy of Berwick-upon-Tweed Borough Council

Market

Berwick has a chartered right to hold two weekly markets on Wednesdays and Saturdays and a fair lasting from Trinity Sunday for eight days. The cattle market used to be held on Hide Hill but in 1887 was removed to a more commodious site outside the Scotch Gate. The egg and butter market was held at the east end of the Town Hall. The fair fell into disuse at the early part of the present century but has been revived and is now opened with much pomp and ceremony.

THE BELL TOWER

BERWICK CHURCH

Photograph courtesy of Berwick-upon-Tweed Borough Council

BERWICK FROM THE OLD CASTLE
Kelso, John Rutherford, Market Place

Salmon Fishing

The salmon has for centuries been the chief commodity of Berwick. At one time they were sent to Newcastle by land. There they were cured and sent to London where they were called Newcastle salmon.

Early in the last century the practice of packing the salmon in ice was started and many ice-houses were built. The introduction of the railway, however, made this unnecessary. The sale of salmon was confined to the salmon coopers of whom there were thirty-six in 1800. The salmon were often very plentiful and we are told "the capture of Salmon in the month of July was prodigious. In a good fishery a boat-load, and sometimes two, are taken in a tide. Once 700 fish were taken in one haul".

Fishery

Today the fishing in the Tweed is controlled by the Berwick Salmon Fisheries Company who employ almost seventy men. The close season is from the 14th September to 15th February and no fishing is allowed from noon on Saturday to Monday morning. There were three modes of fishing in olden times but by the Tweed Fisheries Act of 1857 the wear-shot net is the only one now allowed. The wear-shot net is rowed by means of a boat into the river in a circular form and is immediately drawn to the shore. The mesh must be not less than seven inches round. The net can be of any length but must not block the navigable channel.

Lamberton Toll Bar

Lamberton Toll

The farm of Lamberton forms the south-eastern boundary of Berwickshire. The limits were once shown by a stone dyke which ran from the cliffs overlooking the North Sea to the River Tweed at Paxton. Lamberton lies three miles north of Berwick on the coast road to Edinburgh. The toll here was once famous, like Gretna Green, for Border marriages, which were celebrated well into the second half of the nineteenth century. Many a couple, in order to avoid the expense and delays of a church marriage, have been joined together here for a crown piece and a gill of whiskey. Our sketch on page 38 shows the toll about 1880. Unfortunately the building has recently been demolished.

Lamberton was also famous for the horse racing which once took place here. They are said to have started in the time of James IV of Scotland and continued down to 1837.

Places of Interest near Berwick

Berwick is a good centre for visiting the Scottish Border and the northern part of Northumberland. On the southern side of the Tweed there are many historic places within a few miles of the town. Holy Island, Bamburgh and the Farnes are internationally known. Since we have published separate guides to all these places we will not describe them here. Northumberland is famous for its castles. Those on the coast south of Berwick have been described in our booklet *Northumbrian Castles of the Coast*. However we will describe the greatest of all the Border strongholds, the castle of Norham, which lies seven miles from Berwick. On the journey we pass through the village of East Ord near which is an ancient earthwork. We pass Longridge Towers, a picturesque neo-Tudor mansion built in 1878, until we come to the village of Horncliffe. Nearby is Horncliffe House, a late eighteenth century handsome stone mansion. Continuing our journey we come to the strangely named railway station of Velvet Hall before the great tower of Norham comes into view.

TWEEDMOUTH

Tweedmouth is on the south side of the Tweed opposite Berwick. Founded at an early period it was long used by the English kings as a base of operations against Berwick. Tweedmouth was a portion of the patrimony of St. Cuthbert and continued to belong to the Bishops of Durham until the time of Elizabeth.

There are notices at different times of a small castle at Tweedmouth, probably built by an early Bishop of Durham in connection with the bridge. In 1202 King John wishing to get control of Berwick, then part of Scotland, strengthened this fortress but William the Lion twice destroyed it. During the following centuries it is occasionally mentioned, the last time being in 1753. Its site is unknown.

There was another tower belonging to the hospital of Tweedmouth which stood at Spital. It was built by one of the masters called Bather who was appointed in 1369. In 1612 it was still known as Bathes Tower.

The Tweedmouth "Feast" is a local festival of early religious origin. For many years it lapsed but was revived in 1945. It takes place during the third week in July.

Near the Royal Border Bridge is a small hill called *Hang-a-Dyke Neuk* where Edward III is said to have executed the son of Sir Alexander Seton. The story is uncertain but it appears that during the siege of the town in 1333 Edward had come to an agreement with Sir Alexander Seton for the town to surrender. One of Seton's sons was handed over as a hostage to guarantee good faith. At this moment a relieving Scottish force entered the town and they refused to carry out the terms of surrender. For breach of the agreement Seton's son was hanged in view of the people of Berwick. In Sheldon's *Minstrelsy of the English Border* there is a ballad called "Seton's Sons; or the Beleaguering of Berwicke". According to the ballad Lady Seton was prepared to hand over the keys of the town to save her two sons. Sir Alexander refuses, "Wyth Chryst blessynge, altho they hang my sons, I wolde keep goode fayth wyth the Scottish Kynge and barre out Yedwarde". Preparations are made for the hanging.

> They biggit a gallows on hangie-dyke-neuk,
>   And the hangman came there betyme;
> The cock crow'd loudly o'er the muirs,
>   'Seton's sonnes, 'tis matin pryme'.
>
> The trumpets sounded out oure the Tweed,
>   Wi' a blast o' deadly sound;
> Auld Seton and wyfe goed up on the wa's,
>   For theyre sonnes to death were bound.
>
> They kennt the tread o' their gallant bairns,
>   As they cam forth to die.
> Richard, he mounted the ladder fyrst,
>   And threw himself frae the tree.

William, he was his mither's pride,
And he looked sae bauldly on;
Then kyst his brither's lyefless hands,
When he fand the breath was gone.

He leaped from aff the bitter tree,
And flouchtered in the wynd;
Twa bonnie flowers to wither thus,
And a' for yae man's mind!

Oh! there was a shriek rose in the air,
So wylde, so death-lyke gien;
A mother's wail for her gallant bairns,
Such sight was seldom seen.

It called the grey gull frae the sea,
For he wist his mate had spake.
Never a mither in city walled,
Wi' a heart that wad'nt break.

In the churchyard lies buried John Mackay Wilson, author of the *Tales of the Borders*, and James Stuart, a famous Border character who lived to the great age of 115 years and died in 1844. Although many of the stories told about him are apocryphal he was a remarkable man and of such extraordinary strength that he once carried for a short distance a cart loaded with hay, the total weight being a ton and a half.

Immediately facing the old bridge stood *Tweed House*, an important posting-house on the Great North Road. It is mentioned by Smollett in *Humphrey Clinker*. One of the characters, writing a letter from Tweedmouth, says — "I have now reached the northern extremity of England and see, close to my chamber-window, the Tweed gliding through the arches of that bridge which connects this suburb to the town of Berwick".

Until recently it was thought that this old hostelry had gone, but it has recently been revealed that Tweedmouth House (now an hotel) was the Inn of Smollett. This house is one of the most important buildings in the area and it has been beautifully restored with help from the Department of the Environment. Parts of the building are as old as Berwick's Elizabethan Walls. Two rooms in the building date back to the 16th century and were once the famous Tweedmouth Inn called the Virgin. Outside is a wine and beer cellar at least 400 years old and there is evidence of an earlier convent on the site.

TWEEDMOUTH HOUSE

Spittal

It derives its name from a hospital for lepers, founded there at an early period. It was a fishing village where herring houses once abounded. Just over a century ago it began to develop as a watering-place. In 1657 the Corporation of Berwick bought the Manor of Tweedmouth and Spittal from the Earl of Suffolk for £570, the "best bargain the Corporation ever made".

Spittal was once notorious for its smuggling. "In the old smuggling and buccaneering times it was a great place for landing contraband articles. On a dark night, at a given signal, the lugger stood in for the shore; her boats hoisted out, and her whole cargo landed on the point of Spittal; brawny men would dash into the surf, and in twenty minutes, not a keg or a bale would be seen. The Spittal fishermen were famous smugglers. Lamberton, Mordington and Paxton Tolls (lying on the town boundary) were also notorious depots for smuggling goods and many bladders full of whisky have been carried by the stalwart fishwives from the tolls into Berwick town, to make the burgesses merry with stolen liquor. Various and amusing were the schemes to smuggle in the stuff; and great was the ingenuity and patience displayed by the king's officers to detect the multifarious methods of cheating the revenue". The following interesting story is related about one of the Spittal inns:-

"About twenty years since there was along the frontier an organised gang of coiners, forgers, and smugglers whose operations were conducted on a scale not inferior to what is here described. The chief of the party was one Richard Mendham, a carpenter, who rose to opulence. But he found a short road to wealth, and had taken singular measures for conducting his operations. Amongst these he found means to build in a suburb of Berwick called Spittal a street of small houses, as if for the investment of property. He himself inhabited one of these; another, a species of public-house, was open to his confederates, who held secret and unsuspected communication with him by crossing the roofs of the intervening houses, and descending by a trap-stair, which admitted them into the alcove of the dining-room of Dick Mendham's private mansion. A vault, too, beneath Mendham's stable, was accessible in the manner mentioned in the novel. The post of one of the stalls turned round on a bolt being withdrawn, and gave admittance to a subterranean place of concealment for contraband ......Richard Mendham was tried and executed at Jedburgh".

Norham Castle. 1852

Norham Village

Below the castle is the old village of Norham, which consists of one long, wide street, with a fine green in the middle. On it stands the pinnacled market cross, the lower steps of which are of the thirteenth century. The wind-vane is a fish to commemorate Norham's salmon fishery. Every year on 13th February the vicar stands in a boat on the river at midnight and blesses the opening of the salmon season.

Norham in Saxon times was called *Ubbanford*, i.e. ford of Ubba but by 1050 was called *Northham* which means "north homestead". It was granted to the See of Lindisfarne by King Oswald and about 830 King Ecfrid built a church here, where he reburied the bones of the king and Saint Ceowulph, to whom Bede dedicated his History.

On the site of the Saxon church Bishop Flambard erected a Norman church at the same time as he built the castle. Although much of the Norman work was destroyed during three later restorations there are sufficient remains to show the architectural character of this fine twelfth century building. In the nave are two arcades of round-headed arches, with tall cylindrical columns. In the lofty chancel are five round-headed and deeply-splayed arches in the south wall, connected by a continuous label carved with zigzag. The Norman work also includes the stately chancel arch with three-shafted piers. The south-east window of the chancel, and the wide east window, with its geometrical tracery, belong to the Decorated period.

The church contains two recessed and canopied tombs. The one illustrated here is of fourteenth century workmanship and supports on its slab the stone figure of a knight, clad in mail, his hands clasped, his legs crossed and his feet on a lion. The Puritans removed much of the carving and parts of the figures on the sides. The dark old oak fittings and reredos have come from Durham Cathedral. They were carved after the commonwealth period.

Monumental Effigy in Norham Church

NORHAM CASTLE

Norham, until 1844, was an outlying part of the County Palatine of Durham, and with the shires of Island (including Holy Island and the Farnes) and Bedlington was known as North Durham. Norham was the chief stronghold of this principality. It commanded the chief ford over the Tweed and such was its elevation that from the summit of its keep a wide area of country was under surveillance. It was governed by a constable appointed by the bishop.

Here in 1121 Bishop Flambard ordered a castle to be built. It was almost certainly of the "Motte and Bailey" type with a wooden tower and ditches which correspond to those of the present castle. In 1136, fifteen years after it was built, Norham was taken by David, King of Scotland. It was restored to its owner but two years later war broke out again. This time David razed the castle to the ground.

In 1157 Henry II regained possession of Northumberland and rebuilt in stone the castles of Bamburgh, Newcastle and Wark-upon-Tweed. In the following year Hugh Pudsey, Bishop of Durham built a stone keep at Norham. The architect was Richard of Wolviston a well known Durham builder. The first and second storeys of the keep, parts of the gatehouses to the outer and inner wards, and sections of the curtain walls, survive today from his work.

In 1215 the castle was besieged without success for forty days by Alexander, King of Scotland. In 1318 the Scots blockaded Norham for a whole year and a second siege of seven months in the following year was equally unsuccessful. During the second siege the famous incident of Marmion is supposed to have taken place. Here is the story as told by Leland:- "Aboute this tyme there was a greate feste made yn Lincolnshir, to which cam many gentelmen and ladies; and emonge them one lady brought a heaulme for a man of were, with a very riche creste of gold, to William Marmion, knight, with a lettre of commaundement of her lady, that he should go into the daungerust place in England, and there to let the heaulme to be seene and knownen as famose. So he went to Norham; whither, withyn four days of cumming, cam Philip Moubray, gardian of Berwike, having yn his bande 140 men of armes, the very flour of men of the Scottich marches. Thomas Gray, capitayne of Norham, seying this, brought heis garison afore the barriers of the castel, behynde whom cam William, richely arrayed, as al glittering in gold, and wering the heaulme his lady's present. Then sayd Thomas Gray to Marmion, 'Syr Knight, ye be cum hither to fame your helmet. Mount up on yor horse, and ryde lyke a valiant man to your foes even here at hand, and I forsake God if I rescue not thy body deade or alyve, or I myself wyl dye for it'. Whereapon he toke his cursore, and rode emong the throng of ennemyes, the which layed sore stripes on hym, and pullid hym at the last oute of his sadel to the grounde. Then Thomas Gray with al the hole garison lette prik yn emong the Scottes, and so wondid them, and their horses, that they were over throwen, and Marmyon sore beaten was horsid agayn, and with Gray pursewid the Scottes yn chace. There were taken fifty horses of price, and the wemen of Norham brought them to the foote men to folow the chace".

The incident is used in Bishop Percy's ballad of "The Hermit of Warkworth" and also in Sir Walter Scott's "Marmion". The opening lines of this poem give a graphic description of Norham Castle at sunset.

"Day set on Norham's castled steep,
And Tweed's fair river, broad and deep,
And Cheviot's mountains lone;
The battled towers, the Donjon Keep,
The loopholes grates, where captives weep,
The flanking walls that round it sweep,
In yellow lustre shone.
The warriors on the turrets high,
Moving athwart the evening sky,
Seem'd forms of giant height:
Their armour, as it caught the rays,
Flash'd back again the western blaze,
In lines of dazzling light".

We need not relate in detail Norhan's long eventful history as the "most dangerous" place in England and the "Queen of Border fortresses".

In 1513 James IV invaded England in the campaign which led to the disaster of Flodden. He attacked Norham using the mighty cannon "Mons Meg". The castle was soon in ruins and the garrison surrendered. There is a tradition that the castle was won through the treachery of one of the inmates who advised the king to descend from Ladykirk Band to Gin Haugh, a piece of flat ground near the river and to attack the corner wall there with his cannon.

Norham Castle from the West

"So when the Scots the walls had won
And rifled every nook and place,
The traitor came to the king anon,
But for reward met with disgrace.

"Therefore for this thy traitorous trick
Thou shalt be tried in a trice;
Hangman, therefore,' quoth James, 'be quick;
The groom shall have no better price'."

—*Ballad of Flodden.*

A field north of the castle, called "Hangman's Land", is said to be the place of his execution. The castle was immediately restored and in 1542 Sir Robert Bowes described it as in "very good state, both in reparacions and fortificacions, well furnyshed and stuffed with artyllery, munycions, and other necessaries requysyte to the same". But by 1551 the fortifications were being neglected. The Border Survey describes the castle as "in muche decaye". In 1559 the shires of Norham and Holy Island were taken from the See of Durham. The Lord Warden reported to Lord Cecil in 1580 that if "speedy remedy be not had it will fall flat to the ground". But Queen Elizabeth refused to pay anything for its restoration. The need for the castle had now disappeared.

Description

Norham is laid out as a normal motte and bailey castle but the wards are both larger than usual to accommodate the large garrison and provide quarters for the prince bishop and his retinue when they visited the border. The main entrance is by the *West Gate* (Marmion's Gate). The core of the building is Norman, comprising a tunnel-vaulted entrance with shallow pilasters against the walls. In the fourteenth century it was closed but re-opened in 1404 and provided with a barbican and a drawbridge. The drawbridge pivoted round its centre and when it was raised its inner end sank into a pit which can still be seen under the modern bridge. The *north wall of the Outer Ward* runs along the brink of a steep bank which descends to the Tweed. There are three low arches, built in 1509, which are casements with port-holes for small cannon. Where the wall joins the inner ward is the fifteenth century chapel whose undercroft was converted into a stable in 1521. Only part of this undercroft still stands. The buildings at this point inside the moat are partly connected with washing and partly with the flooding of the moat.

The Inner Ward is entered by a modern bridge which is on the site of its medieval predecessor. The gateway is in poor condition. Against the north wall is the Great Hall of Norham Castle which was rebuilt early in the sixteenth century. The adjoining Great Chamber is contemporary. As usual the kitchen (with its oven). pantry and buttery are at the screens passage end of the Hall.

The Keep measured eithty-four by sixty feet and was originally three storeys high and its high-pitched roof line can be traced on its

THE SOUTH-EAST VIEW OF NORHAM CASTLE.

THIS Castle was built by Ralph Bp: of Durham, on the top of a steep Rock moated round & fortify'd with several strong Walls; for the better security of this part of his Diocess against the frequent incursions of the Scots Moss=Troopers; it being on the Brink of the River Tweed Bordering, Scotland: it hath often been of great service to England and this Lords, who were ever at War: or rather; so that the English kept it very well fortify'd; in the Reign of K. H.7. this K. of Scots being at this castle for many days; untill he dispar'd of a conquest, rais'd this Siege, & retreated. in K. H.8. Reign James, K. of Scotland attacked it with so oten men; but the Governour renting Ammunition after 6 Days: brave residence surrendred it to the K: but it was soon regain'd by the E: of Surry, who was afterwards created E: of Norfolk & L.d Howard his son E: of Worcester: I. & R. Buck delin. et sculp. 1728.

To William Orde Esq.r: Owner of
This Castle This Prospect is humbly Inscrib'd by
His oblig'd humble Serv.ts S. & N. Buck.

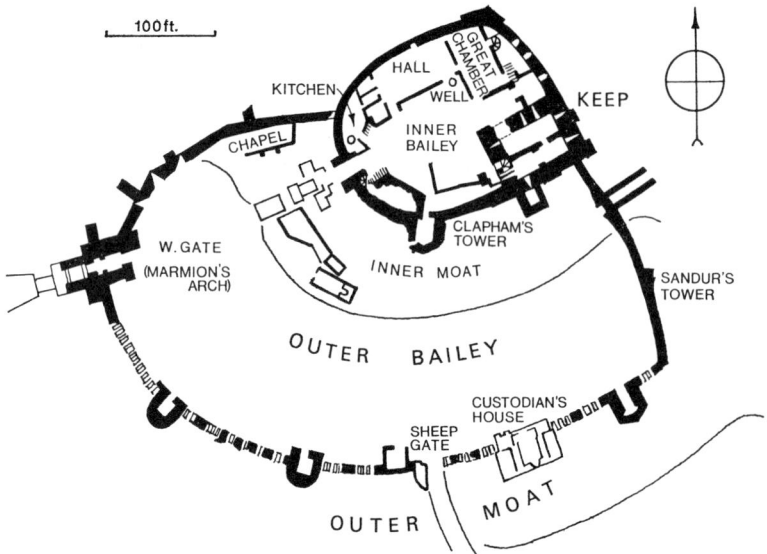

PLAN OF NORHAM CASTLE

east wall. In 1422-25 the keep was rebuilt from the second storey upwards to a height of five storeys and a spiral staircase added. The Norman keep was divided unequally by a cross-wall. The south half of the basement is barrel vaulted, the north half has early Norman rubble vault of four bays with big flat unmoulded transverse ribs springing from pilasters. In Norman times the keep was entered by an external staircase on the first floor from which entrance to the basement was possible. On the first floor is a Norman fireplace in the south wall and a magnificent arched niche at the east end.

On the south side of the inner ward is *Clapham's Tower*. It has a pointed front and portholes for artillery. It was built early in the sixteenth century. The neighbouring oblong tower is of fifteenth century construction. The *east side of the Outer Wall* is Norman work and the Sandur's Tower was added probably in the thirteenth century. The original south curtain wall of the outer ward was probably for long only a wooden palisade and ditch. The round-fronted turrets were built in the thirteenth century, the polygonal turret with well-preserved gunports is of sixteenth century workmanship as is its companion on the west. In front of the *Sheep Gate* was once a wide moat. The upper storey was used as the constable's lodging. In the south curtain wall are several mysterious arches. The only suggestion for their use is that they were the foundations of a stone curtain wall built on an earlier earth wall.